THE LITTLE GREEN BOOK OF
FINANCIAL HAPPINESS

RAYMAR RODRIGUEZ

authorHOUSE®

AuthorHouse™
1663 Liberty Drive
Bloomington, IN 47403
www.authorhouse.com
Phone: 1-800-839-8640

Major financial decisions should be consulted with an appropriate attorney or tax advisor. This book is not intended to give the reader tax or legal advice.

Published by AuthorHouse 08/26/2013

ISBN: 978-1-4918-1206-8 (sc)
ISBN: 978-1-4918-1205-1 (hc)
ISBN: 978-1-4918-1204-4 (e)

Library of Congress Control Number: 2013915150

I deeply appreciate all the assistance and support from my family and friends. They have helped me during the book writing process and have been extremely supportive of my project. All were involved in the reviewing and revising multiple steps of my first book. I especially appreciate the patience and thoughtfulness that went into everyone's review and constructive criticism.

My deepest gratitude is to my wife who not only assisted in the entire process, but put up with my eternal questioning of every step of this book.

This book is dedicated to my three children whom have and will continue to assist me. My deepest wish is that they learn from the book writing process, the promotion of the book and all the different aspects that making a successful book entails. Hopefully they will gain the truest sense of FINANCIAL HAPPINESS in the process.

Contents

FOREWORD

Be the change you wish to see in the world.—Mahatma Gandhi

My husband wrote the Financial Happiness books to help others overcome their financial struggles by searching for the true meaning of their happiness within their financial means. By letting go of things outside our control, we see the true value of life. This was a personal journey for him and our family. He has taught a financial workshop for years and felt the need to share it with others because it may bring others joy and financial happiness.

This book was written with the idea that people might not have to fall so hard, if someone had extended a loving or helping hand, or offered a simple word of advice. Anyone can change someone else's life with just one sentence at the right time and place.

Happiness, whether financial or by itself, might serve as a deterrent from a deepening hatred of life itself. A person who is content with his life is less likely to be destructive and fall for the false promises of illegally attained wealth and its trappings. This book will give the reader a guide to a simpler and more fulfilling life that he or she already has within.

This book provides a simple way to look at personal finances. Everything we need or want is measured in terms of money. Money issues are one of the leading causes of divorce in our society. Money and material life in general place many pressures on all members of society. Why? We tend to measure everything, even our sense of happiness, in terms of dollars. The ability to understand and manage a personal budget gives one a fighting chance at attaining financial happiness. This little book will guide the reader on a road to a better life by learning how to control his or her money and not allowing their money to control them.

Jacqueline Q. Rodriguez

INTRODUCTION

While working at a bank, I met a woman who said she was having a horrible day. She complained that she was expecting to be laid off from work the following day. She had worked for the same company for thirty-two years, and they were replacing her with younger people at a much lower pay scale. She'd been a model employee all her life. She had never taken a day off, had never abused a sick day, and had always been faithful to her employer. She was extremely upset. She told me there was no happiness in her life.

I asked her one question: What is one thing that really makes you happy? She said it was spending a day at the beach. When I asked her when the last time was that she'd gone to the beach, she responded that it had been four years. I asked her why, and she gave me ten different excuses. When she finished with her excuses, I told her how cheap parking was at Miami Beach, which was only thirty minute drive from her home. I told her if she was getting fired tomorrow, she should take a day off, go to the beach and enjoy it, and then go to work the following day with more positive and relaxed attitude.

She took that day off and spent the whole afternoon reading a book at the beach. When she returned to work on Friday, her boss told her she looked relaxed and healthy, that she did not look like someone who had been sick the day before. He also told her the whole office was falling apart because she'd been out. Apparently, she was more needed than she thought, and she did not lose her job that day.

How we look at our challenges will determine how we live. Find happiness wherever you can, and make your life revolve around things that bring you joy, happiness, and peace. Focus on those things, and everything else will fall into place.

This book will help you on your path to financial happiness. The effort you put into it will determine your success. After finishing this little book, you will have a different perspective on the true value of your life and money.

CHAPTER 1

FINANCIAL HAPPINESS EXPLAINED

Don't save what is left after spending; spend what is left after saving.—Warren Buffett

Financial happiness is nothing more than living within your means and seeing a constant improvement in your finances. Steady and constant improvements in cash flow create happiness and a sense of accomplishment. The ability to regularly improve your quality of life, to purchase items and services you desire with minimal effort, and to save money with relative ease are extremely fulfilling. This happiness comes from the ability to spend, save, donate, or give away disposable funds. These actions create a true sense of wealth.

This book is designed to create awareness and happiness within your current financial reality. The book is meant to be read over a two-week period, approximately ten to fifteen minutes a day, while maintaining a basic set of calculations and forms. Once you finish this book, you will have a good idea of your current financial situation. The book will allow you to plan a series of small, incremental improvements toward your finances and cash flow.

This book is not a get-rich-quick scheme. It is a compilation of tried and true exercises that can create a positive outlook of your personal finances and budget.

The better a person understands his or her budget, the easier it is to make changes to improve the situation. A budget or improvement plan starts with gathering your financial information. Constantly fine-tuning a budget will increase cash flow or spendable cash, reduce debt, and increase savings.

I often hear, "I cannot better my finances since I earn very little," "I can never save since all my income goes out as soon as it arrives," or, "Budgets are for the rich." A good budget and plan can help everyone, but it's always easier to complain instead of getting to work.

A budget is just a one-step-at-a-time process. I have been teaching a financial survival class in Miami for several years, and it was nicknamed "**SCUBA SFL**." **SCUBA SFL** had nothing to do with scuba diving or South Florida.

SCUBA SFL stands for

S=Seeking help

C="Cash flowing" your personal finances

U=Understanding what caused your problems

B=Budgeting your income and expenses

A=Accepting and applying the needed changes to improve your situation

S=Savings

F=Forgiveness (because without forgiving yourself and anyone you blame for your current situation, nothing will ever change)

L=Love (the magical element that makes sacrifices possible)

I am a person of faith. I love the concept of calling GOD Abba. I picture myself as a helpless baby calling out to my father to help me with my most crucial of needs. I truly believe praying and asking for divine intervention gives you the strength to find the energy to improve your finances and rediscover the joys of life. Prayer and meditation, in times of trouble, give the faithful an edge to overcome the most devastating of situations.

Bad finances are mostly transitional in nature and can be overcome with planning and a little work.

The underlying idea of this book is that financial happiness is easy to attain. Financial happiness is the opposite of the stress, frustration, and anger that is felt by most people dealing with money problems. Your finances do not have to be a bad thing. This book is designed to guide you, the reader, on a set of small changes that will improve your finances.

1. The first step is not counting your pennies but writing down the things in life that truly make you happy.
2. The second step is to understand your exact financial situation in detail. The answers might shock you and open your eyes to your reality.
3. The third step will require a little reading and filling out a few forms over the next few weeks.
4. The fourth step will be creating a budget—yes, a formal budget!

The checklist to financial happiness will guide you. The financial happiness progress tracker will allow you to measure your success.

Everyone has a budget. They might not understand it, but they have a budget. Have you ever tried to purchase groceries with your credit or debit card, and the transaction was rejected? That was the budget you did not know you had screaming for help.

If you declared bankruptcy, that was your old budget, which died. Your final discharge from bankruptcy was the burial. "Bankruptcy" was created for when a budget becomes overwhelmed and dies. Thankfully there is a legal process for it in the United States and in many other countries.

If you just received your discharge, congratulations—you are the proud parent of a brand new baby budget. Please understand that your old budget died, not you. The government created the bankruptcy process to free you from your overwhelming debt, not to punish you. The purpose of the bankruptcy is to make you a better member of society. You are now free from your old debts and accounts, forgiven in my eyes, the government's eyes, and your creditors' eyes. Now forgive yourself and all those you blame for your bankruptcy, and let's get to work.

Your new budget will be like a beautiful baby, full of love and hope. Just like a new child it requires work, effort, and attention.

Whether you filed for bankruptcy or not, the forgiveness part has probably not sunk in yet. It is very important that you forgive yourself. If you do not, it will be difficult to free yourself of your past budgetary mistakes. I promise that if you truly forgive yourself, the pain, guilt, shame, and hopelessness will quickly fade. The hope of a new budget and a better future will help you on the path to your financial happiness.

My faith tells me that only God can forgive us. Organized religions have many rituals based on that concept. Letting go of your past mistakes is also a form of forgiveness. The hardest person to forgive is usually you. Forgiveness is very vast then. The concepts and implications are too deep and complicated to cover in this book. A murderer, rapist, thief or bank robber must also seek forgiveness to continue growing and improving their lives. A criminal must seek forgiveness from his victims, society, God and himself/herself.

Seeking forgiveness will give you a peace of mind that you are truly trying to better yourself. You cannot change the past, but you can strive to better the present and the future. A clean slate is a wonderful thing. You can decide only to put good things on it and dream of ways to make life better. Tackling your problems whether financial, emotional or criminal with an open heart and an open mind will give you a better chance of overcoming the problem.

This book deals with problems in budgeting and personal finance. If you dig deep enough most financial problems are created by issues not related to money at all. You cannot solve a problem until you understand the problem.

Let us now try to figure out your true numbers.

First let's complete the net worth balance sheet to figure out your true net worth.

Second, we'll figure out your actual cash flow on the savings worksheet.

Third, we will plug in the numbers in the first unit of your financial happiness progress tracker.

Your first calculations will probably be a little off, which is okay. You will repeat this exercise in great detail in a few days. You must get comfortable with your finances, and this process will get you accustomed to fine tuning your budgets as income and expenses change.

On the path to financial happiness, you will find additional sources of income. You will start eliminating certain expenses and start adding deposits to different bank accounts.

As your budget progress accelerates, you will spend less, save more, and change or eliminate certain expenses from your monthly budget.

Journaling is a tool used in many levels of school. Keeping a journal has many positive benefits. It can help with personal growth, problem-solving, etc. You will notice a lot of empty spaces in this book, which have been added so you can take notes if you wish. Write down ideas and make calculations. This book is meant to be used and written in.

I wish that the book will eventually be all marked up and all the forms filled out. After a few months of using this book and noticing your real progress, buying a few clean copies to have or give away will be easy. This book is just a tool to get you to that place called financial happiness.

Spend a little time working on your net worth balance sheet and your CASHFLOW worksheet. Then please put the book down and to allow yourself some time to think about all that makes you happy.

Please only use numbers from memory and what you think these numbers are. Please do not pull out statements and bills just yet.

Let's get started.

Savings/Cash-Flow Worksheet

The blank spaces are for specific expenses of your personal budget.

	1st Estimate	2nd Estimate Date	3rd Estimate Date	4th Estimate Date	5th Estimate Date
Savings Deposit					
Mortgage					
2nd Mortgage (if applicable)					
Home Insurance					
Property Taxes					
Monthly HOA (Home Owners Association)					
Maintenance					
Maintenance					
Electricity					
Utility 1					
Utility 2					
Grocery					
Casual Dining					
Lunch					
Gas					
Day Care					
School Tuition					
School Loan					
Car Loan					

Car Loan					
Car Insurance					
Total Expenses	1st Estimate				
Sources of income	Description				
Income 1					
Income 2					
Total Income					
Total Income/ Total Expenses = CASHFLOW					

If your CASHFLOW number is greater than zero, your budget is balanced. Fine-tuning your budget is all you need.

If your CASHFLOW number is negative or less than zero, you are taking on debt every month to maintain your lifestyle. I am happy that you have this book in your hands.

Most people leave the first category (Savings Deposit) blank. Paying yourself first is a very difficult concept for many people to understand. A simple $20.00 weekly deposit into a savings account or an empty coffee can turn into a $1000.00 balance in the course of just one year.

BALANCE SHEET WORKSHEET

The blank spaces are for specific assets and liabilities of your personal budget.

Assets	1st Estimate	2nd Estimate	3rd Estimate
Home			
Property			
Car			
Cash			
Checking			
Savings			
401(k), Pension, 403(b), etc.			
IRA			
Life Insurance Cash Value			
Annuity			
Personal Property			
Total Assets			
Liabilities			
Mortgage			
2nd Mortgage			
3rd Mortgage			
Credit Card			
Credit Card			
Credit Card			

Other Loan			
Total Liabilities			
Total Assets/Total Liabilities = Net Worth			
Net Worth			

Please be realistic when placing a value on an item. Market value is the price an item could be sold relatively quickly. For example, a home you paid $300,000 for five years ago but would sell for $150,000 should now be entered at $150,000. Use the same rule of thumb with vehicles and personal property.

A growing positive net worth is the goal of financial happiness. It does not matter how small the increase in wealth is, just that it is growing. Every day that passes and you have a few extra more dollars to your name, you are richer.

If your net worth is a large negative number, you might be *broke*. It might be time to seek out an attorney to review your options. Many people with large amounts of student debt might fall into this category and not be broke at all. Your education and your ability to earn a good and consistent income are your most valuable assets. You have not counted or valued your education as part of your net worth calculations. There are many calculators to value an education and the earning potential of an individual on the web. Let's keep reading.

CHAPTER 2

WHAT IS THE IMPORTANCE
OF A BUDGET?

Budgets, planning, loans, interest rates, payments, incomes, and cash flows should all be considered during a financial review. Most families do not have a financial budget or even balance their checking accounts. Rough calculations are all that are usually generated, and usually after a problem occurs.

The detection of problems is usually brought to light when the balance of the bank account goes negative, a credit card balance surpasses the credit limit, or a collection call comes in. This is crisis-mode budgeting, an activity that does not lend itself to longer-term planning or a formal budget.

In the following process you will get to know yourself a little better. The process will remind you of what makes you happy and some of your forgotten dreams.

Please answer the following questions. It is not a race, so if you cannot honestly answer them, take time to think about them. Speak to an old friend or a family member. If you are working with your spouse or partner on this journey to financial happiness, the questions make for great dinner conversation. Enjoy this activity. It will give you strength and inspiration to start working on improving your finances.

There are no right or wrong answers. This exercise will allow you to know yourself better. Over the next few weeks, review your answers—modify and update them. I have added a few blank pages for you to write down your answers, notes, and ideas. You will start to notice that money is not the only component to financial happiness.

The Big Questions regarding Your Search for Financial Happiness

1. What really makes me happy?
2. What event in my life brings me memories of total happiness?
3. What do I dream about?
4. What do I want to own/have/use?
5. What are my top ten happiest memories?
6. Was abundant money the reason for my ten happiest memories?
7. What keeps me up at night?
8. What are my happiest childhood memories?

Happiness

Happiness

Happiness

_____

_____

_____

_____

_____

_____

_____

_____

_____

_____

_____

_____

_____

_____

_____

_____

_____

_____

_____

_____

_____

_____

_____

_____

Happiness

I apologize from the bottom of my heart if this exercise brought up painful memories. Please call someone for help—a psychologist, a friend, a family member, a hotline, a priest, a pastor, a rabbi, an imam. Just call someone. Help is closer than you think. Please accept my sincere wishes that you find help and happiness.

CHAPTER 3

THE BASICS

This book is based on my opinions, studies, and personal journey. I generated my thinking about finances over twelve years of dealing with individuals as a banker and investment adviser. I reviewed thousands of budgets over my career, and my experiences were very consistent.

The more *details* a budget has, the deeper one can dig and search for problems or opportunities in the budget itself.

To improve your cash flow you must understand your incomes and expenses.

Cash flow is the net dollar amount that can be spent, saved, or invested.

By having the details of your budget in front of you, you can analyze where your money is spent. Knowing your expenses, level of savings, and cash-flow amount are important. It allows for analysis and adjustment that can lead to improvement in your overall finances.

Breaking down your expenses by categories is an important task. You can then pinpoint problem areas or items where additional savings can be attained. For example, after a quick glance at your monthly budget, you notice your cable bill is $230 a month versus the $65 you expected to see. You start there.

Ask yourself: Why is this bill so high? Can this bill be reduced, substituted, or eliminated, or is the price fair?

This exercise should be done with every item in your budget. The savings you find is yours to spend or save. That is just a little extra motivation.

Items to focus on:

- o Cell phone bills
- o Food choices
- o Cable bills
- o Electrical bills
- o Water bill
- o Vacations
- o Online/Internet services
- o Lunches (casual dining)
- o Insurance policies (auto, home, life, health)
- o Basic services (lawn, dry cleaning, babysitting/day care)
- o Luxury items/vices/habits
- o Donations/gifts/hobbies and collections

Our standard of living is directly related to how we spend our money. Our society, the media, and our commercialized economy place a lot of emphasis on wealth. The ways in which we live, look, dress, drive, smell, and spend our money are shaped by the society we live in. The lives of the rich and famous are always in the limelight, and the masses tend to aspire to pursue certain luxuries even when they cannot afford them. Good marketers never lose the chance to link a famous athlete's performance with an expensive pair of sneakers or his cool $80 team jersey.

What is aspirational wealth?

Aspirational wealth is the search for the appearance of wealth. Aspirational wealth is the façade of true wealth. It is the consumption by people of lesser means of expensive items and luxury services normally marketed to the wealthy.

Aspirational wealth is a huge influence in the way we spend our money. Aspirational wealth is at the epicenter of the current recession or financial readjustment that we are living in. Understanding your finances will allow you to enjoy your life better. Controlling your budget and cash flow will allow you to make honest choices. A financial plan handled with frugality and a humble heart will give you a truly rich and rewarding life.

A well-organized and honest budget will allow you to avoid the trappings of excessive materialism and economic suffrage. If you still want a $200 pair of sneakers and feel they will bring you happiness, buy them. The trick is to budget for them and hopefully get them on sale.

Items of Aspirational Wealth I Spend Money on and How Much I Spend

Item   **Amount Spent**

_____   _____

_____   _____

_____   _____

_____   _____

_____   _____

_____   _____

_____   _____

_____   _____

_____   _____

_____   _____

_____   _____

_____   _____

_____   _____

_____   _____

_____   _____

_____   _____

_____   _____

Before you start filling out any part of the forms, please gather three to six months' worth of bank statements, receipts, bills, and payments to create a better and more detailed budget. Use the same forms that you filled out in the first chapter, but this time use the exact numbers of your real expenses and incomes.

In the process you will get to know yourself—what makes you happy, your assets, your liabilities, your faults, and your strengths. Think of this for a while. Start taking notes while going through your papers, accounts, statements, etc.

You will then fill out the forms provided next as clean copies or downloaded from our website. Be thorough; the more detail, the better.

Please note and highlight every item in your budget that was different from your first estimation.

After reading a chapter, let the basic concepts sink in and ponder what you just read. Make adjustments constantly to your basic budget. A plan as important as your personal budget deserves attention. The more you put into it, the more you will get out of it.

Savings/Cash-Flow Worksheet

	1st Estimate	2nd Estimate Date	3rd Estimate Date	4th Estimate Date	5th Estimate Date
Savings Deposit					
Mortgage					
2nd Mortgage (if applicable)					
Home Insurance					
Property Taxes					
Monthly HOA (Home Owners Association)					
Maintenance					
Maintenance					
Electricity					
Utility 1					
Utility 2					
Grocery					
Casual Dining					
Lunch					
Gas					
Day Care					
School Tuition					

School Loan					
Car Loan					
Car Loan					
Car Insurance					
Total Expenses	1st Estimate				
Sources of income	Description				
Income 1					
Income 2					
Total Income					
Total Income/ Total Expenses = CASHFLOW					

Please date your worksheet on each attempt. It will help you fine tune your budget and progress.

Balance Sheet
Net Worth Worksheet

Assets	1st Date	2nd Date	3rd Date
Home			
Property			
Car			
Cash			
Checking			
Savings			
401(k), Pension, 403(b), etc.			
IRA			
Life Insurance Cash Value			
Annuity			
Personal Property			
Total Assets			
Liabilities			
Mortgage			
2nd Mortgage			
3rd Mortgage			
Credit Card			
Credit Card			
Credit Card			

Loan			
Total Liabilities			
Total Assets/Total Liabilities = Net Worth			

Notes

Notes

Financial success and happiness is also a state of mind, not just a cold mathematical formula. It is all about finding a balance between your incomes and your outflows. You always want to earn more money than you spend. In reality, it is harder to earn money. Our world is full of reasons and excuses to spend money you do not have. Your budget and the discipline to follow it can take a long time to master. Once you dominate the basic concepts and activities in this book, you should be able to start your path to financial happiness.

Let's review the checklist to financial happiness. You might have many items on the list under control, so just check them off. This list is not absolute; add your individual goals and create realistic savings targets. As you advance on your journey, review the list, update it, and make changes. It is your list to financial happiness.

Having time to go fishing makes me very happy. I love fishing so much it does not matter to me if I catch fish or not. Some people I know hate going fishing. I cannot pay them enough to go with me.

Allow yourself to think about the activities in life that truly bring you joy and happiness. The following pages are set aside for your notes, thoughts and comments.

What do you love to do?

What do you truly enjoy?

What is stopping you from doing the activities you love?

How much money or time do you need to fulfill them?

Are they realistic?

Checklists of Financial Happiness

Please review the following four lists. The lists are only a guide and are not mandatory or absolute in any way. They are set up only to assist you on your journey to Financial Happiness. Some of you will find steps that do not apply to you, please skip them. You will also be able to add your own goals. Space has been set aside for your modifications. Read the lists a few times to get an idea of the flow of the four checklists before you start making notations. Check off items that you have achieved. If dollar amounts are available, please plug them in the provided spaces. Revisit regularly your Checklists of Financial Happiness and enjoy your progress. You might see a confusing puzzle at first but as you work with the checklists they will start making sense.

The dreams, targets, and goals are yours. Accept some of the basic ideas and adjust the rest to yourself, your wishes, your dreams and your goals. Letters A through F in all the lists are left blank for your own categories and goals.

_____

_____

_____

_____

_____

_____

_____

_____

_____

_____

_____

_____

_____

_____

_____

_____

_____

"Happiness" - Checklist

Do you know what makes you happy?_____

How happy are you?_____

Create a list of your favorite free or almost free activities that you enjoy.

_____

Are you enjoying those free activities? _____

Assess your happiness?_____

What free activities are you not enjoying? Why?_____

_____

Is your faith playing a role in your search for happiness?_____

Is your spouse/partner on your same journey to Financial Happiness?

_____

Are you speaking to others about improving their finances?_____

Celebrate three months of budgeting._____

Are you finding dignity and additional strength from the sacrifices you are making on the search for Financial Happiness?_____

_____

Re-assess your happiness?_____

Is this book helpful on your search for Financial Happiness?_____

Celebrate six months of budgeting?_____

Are you sharing your happiness with other?_____

Celebrate one year of budgeting!_____

Are you helping others find their happiness?_____

Are you giving to those you wish to help?_____

Are you seeing improvements in your overall attitude towards money, your future, and your happiness?_____

_____

Are you enjoying your daily work more?_____

Are you enjoying spending your left over money after allocating funds to savings?_____

Are you noticing that Financial Happiness is possible?_____

A)

B)

C)

D)

E)

F)

_____

_____

_____

_____

_____

_____

Financial Happiness achieved! _____ Date _____

"Living within your means" - Checklist

Fill out: Preliminary cash-flow budget and balance sheet._____

_____

Are you broke or not? _____

_____

If broke, you need to see a bankruptcy attorney. _____

_____

Accept your financial situation._____

_____

Create a plan to improve your basic situation._____

Start controlling your expenses._____

Do the first cash flow and balance sheet re-do._____

Search for savings in your monthly budget._____

Are you living beyond your means?_____

Search for additional sources of income._____

Cut monthly services that you are not using or cannot afford._____

_____

Second cash-flow budget and balance sheet re-do._____

What can you do to adjust your standard of living?_____

_____

Create a long term budget plan. _____

_____

Search for more monthly savings in your budget._____

Plan a low cost vacation._____

A)

B)

C)

D)

E)

F)

_____

_____

_____

_____

_____

_____

_____

_____

_____

_____

_____

I'm living within my means! _____ date _____

"Savings" - Checklist

This checklist will record the growth of your money. Never worry that your progress is slow. Every dollar counts and a bucket can be filled one drop at a time. Adjust the numbers to your budget.

1 Open your first regular savings account._____

2 Open an emergency savings account

3 Set up a cash stash at home (coffee can, a little box or an envelope).

4 Reach a savings goal of a number of months of income (your month income is $_____).

For example : a "2" would represent 2 months of income saved.

5 Finding savings in reduction of your monthly expenses._____

6 Opening a mutual fund or another investment._____

7 Open an IRA or retirement fund_____

8 Prepay a major purchase_____

9 Leave grocery store with money you were planning on spending because you used coupons, took advantage of sales, etc._____

_____

10 You did not spend all the money at a store you were planning to spend. You got a better deal than you expected and decided not to spend the extra cash but save it._____

_____

11 Purchase life insurance_____

12 Save for college for your children_____

13 Purchase precious metal to diversify assets. (gold, silver, platinum)

_____

14 Have children's education fully funded._____

15 Save for a major repair or replacement of durable item._____

16 Save for a newer car._____

17 Save for a down payment for a home_____

18 Understanding your finances after retirement._____

19 Have retirement fully funded._____

20 Down payment for a home or an investment achieved._____

_____

A)

B)

C)

D)

E)

F)

_____

_____

_____

_____

_____

_____

_____

_____

_____

_____

Saving money has become a way of life for me. _____ date _____

"Reducing debt" - Checklist

Starting point of this list is to know the amounts and types of your total debt.

Car loan 1 _____ Car loan 2 _____ Mortgage _____

Equity Line _____ Credit card 1 _____ Credit card 2 _____

Credit card 3 _____ Credit card 4 _____

Loan1 _____ Loan 2 _____ Loan 3 _____

A) _____ / _____ B) _____/_____ C) _____/_____

D) _____/_____ E) _____/_____ F) _____/_____

The letters A through F, will allow you to add debt categories not listed. The goal of this checklist is to guide you in the elimination of your debt. A mortgage is long term debt and normally cannot be eliminated overnight. Start by eliminating the highest interest credit cards and personal loans first. Review your total amount of debt every month. Record dollar amount and date of each major change in a particular debt. (For example: Credit card 1 started with a balance of $1300 the first day of the checklist and now it has a balance of $850.) You would record it as:

$800- 07 /31/13	$650- 09/15/13	$430 -11/12/13

Credit card 1_____

Credit card 2_____

Credit card 3_____

Credit card 4_____

Home equity line_____

Loan 1_____

Loan 2_____

Loan 3_____

Home mortgage_____

A)

B)

C)

D)

E)

F)

You paid off your home! _____ date _____

You are debt free! _____ date _____

Treat yourself to something you have always wanted without worrying about money!

_____date_____

Notes on Happiness

Notes on Happiness

Notes, Comments, Ideas...

Notes, Comments, Ideas...

Savings/Cash-Flow Worksheet

	1st Estimate	2nd Estimate Date	3rd Estimate Date	4th Estimate Date	5th Estimate Date
Savings Deposit					
Mortgage					
2nd Mortgage (if applicable)					
Home Insurance					
Property Taxes					
Monthly HOA (Home Owners Association)					
Maintenance					
Maintenance					
Electricity					
Utility 1					
Utility 2					
Grocery					
Casual Dining					
Lunch					
Gas					
Day Care					
School Tuition					
School Loan					
Car Loan					
Car Loan					

Car Insurance					
Total Expenses	1st Estimate				
Sources of income	Description				
Income 1					
Income 2					
Total Income					
Total Income/ Total Expenses = CASHFLOW					

Please date your worksheet on each attempt. It will help you fine tune your budget and progress.

Each column represents one month. Hopefully your expense items will decrease and your income will stay the same or increase. You will see how the numbers change from month to month. Every few dollars you save in a particular expense category can be transferred to your savings. Ideally, every expense item decreases a few dollars and your savings portion increases.

Please review and start fine-tuning this budget every few weeks for the next few months.

Start looking for areas in your budget to save a few dollars. For example, eliminate your landline or services you do not use, such as call waiting. If you notice that you speak more on your cell phone than on your home phone, or the only people who call you at home are collection agencies, consider disconnecting the landline.

Net Worth

Assets			
Home			
Property			
Property			
Car			
Car			
Car			
Cash			
Checking			
Savings			
401(k), Pension, 403(b), etc.			
IRA			
Life Insurance Cash Value			
Annuity			
Total Assets			
Liabilities			
Mortgage			
2nd Mortgage			
3rd Mortgage			
Credit Card			
Credit Card			
Credit Card			
Loan			
Net Worth			

We need to attempt to increase the bottom line called net worth. It can be done in two ways increasing the assets or their values or reducing your debt. Attempt to increase your net worth in two ways: reducing your debt and increasing your assets. Try to do this exercise every few months and record the results on the financial happiness progress tracker.

Savings allows for a family budget to survive a downturn in income. Over a course of a lifetime of regular savings, a family of humble means can amass a fortune. The additional earnings from interest payments, dividends, and capital gains on exchanges all enhance a regular saving program.

Expense log: Please start to track everything you spend, whether paid with cash, credit card, check, debit card, or money order. The book has enough space to handle about two months of expenses. The rear of the book has an additional expense log, and you may download additional forms online. The website to download these forms is in progress. Please visit, and keep checking back.

Expense Log

Date	Description	Location were purchased	Amount

Expense Log

Date	Description	Location were purchased	Amount
_____	_____	_____	_____
_____	_____	_____	_____
_____	_____	_____	_____
_____	_____	_____	_____
_____	_____	_____	_____
_____	_____	_____	_____
_____	_____	_____	_____
_____	_____	_____	_____
_____	_____	_____	_____
_____	_____	_____	_____
_____	_____	_____	_____
_____	_____	_____	_____
_____	_____	_____	_____
_____	_____	_____	_____
_____	_____	_____	_____

Expense Log

Date	Description	Location were purchased	Amount
_____	_____	_____	_____
_____	_____	_____	_____
_____	_____	_____	_____
_____	_____	_____	_____
_____	_____	_____	_____
_____	_____	_____	_____
_____	_____	_____	_____
_____	_____	_____	_____
_____	_____	_____	_____
_____	_____	_____	_____
_____	_____	_____	_____
_____	_____	_____	_____
_____	_____	_____	_____
_____	_____	_____	_____
_____	_____	_____	_____
_____	_____	_____	_____

Expense Log

Date	Description	Location were purchased	Amount
_____	_____	_____	_____
_____	_____	_____	_____
_____	_____	_____	_____
_____	_____	_____	_____
_____	_____	_____	_____
_____	_____	_____	_____
_____	_____	_____	_____
_____	_____	_____	_____
_____	_____	_____	_____
_____	_____	_____	_____
_____	_____	_____	_____
_____	_____	_____	_____
_____	_____	_____	_____
_____	_____	_____	_____
_____	_____	_____	_____
_____	_____	_____	_____

Expense Log

Date	Description	Location were purchased	Amount

CHAPTER 4

LET'S TALK SAVING

Savings is money that is put away for a rainy day. Many books, classes, and lectures claim that saving 10 percent of your salary is a good place to start. Some people will have the ability to save much more. Others will struggle with hitting the 10 percent mark. People who cannot save 10 percent will give a thousand excuses why. They will say that they do not earn enough. They will blame the high price of gasoline and food.

The most important person to pay first every week is you. This is a concept that is fundamental to this program. Never short-change or lie to yourself. You must protect yourself and your family, and saving will be a powerful guard in that task.

Savings is more than just a set figure on a balance sheet or a budget. It is a concept that must be accepted and practiced. People who save too much are called extreme savers, cheapskates, misers, hoarders, and even some other very negative names. Saving does not have to be stressful and should not have negative connotations.

Saving is deferred gratification. It is necessary for a budget that is being set up to include a savings component. For some people, the concept of saving is easy. They earn $100 a week and automatically put $10 into savings. This is regular savings in its simplest form.

Other people only like to save special sources of income, such as a year-end bonus or a tax refund. The problem with this type of specific saving is that if the person only saves special income, when an unexpected or major expense occurs, they automatically consume the majority of their savings. Why? They never planned for the unexpected expense into their budget. A good budget and financial plan should have regular savings, emergency savings, and retirement savings.

In 2013, four tires for a car or an SUV cost between $400 and $1,000. A damaged transmission or a blown engine could cost between $800 and $5,000. A new roof can cost between $5,000 and $35,000. A funeral can cost between $4,000 and $8,000. Emergencies are just unexpected expenses, and an emergency savings account is created to meet those needs.

If a person does not have any savings, then he or she is forced to use credit cards, loans, or some other higher-cost provider who offers financing as part of their business model. A super saver and planner would say, "I will need $600 for four new tires for my car next year. I need to save $50 a month to have the money saved by the time the tires need to be purchased next year." The super saver will also be on the lookout for any major coupons or promotions.

A quick comment on savings: start immediately. Find a few dollars and put them in a jar, an empty coffee can, or an old book. You now have a new savings program. You are now the owner of the *first bank of your family*—and no one needs to know.

Flash Saving Exercise

Try to find $ _____ (for example, $125)
of savings in ten regular monthly expenses.

	Expense	Description	Normal Cost	Monthly Savings
1.	_____	_____	_____	_____
2.	_____	_____	_____	_____
3.	_____	_____	_____	_____
4.	_____	_____	_____	_____
5.	_____	_____	_____	_____
6.	_____	_____	_____	_____
7.	_____	_____	_____	_____
8.	_____	_____	_____	_____
9.	_____	_____	_____	_____
10.	_____	_____	_____	_____

Total Savings Found: _____

Do this exercise every month for a few months (up to six times). You will be amazed at how often you will find a new way to save or an item (expense) that you can reduce or altogether eliminate.

CHAPTER 5

SHOPPING

Before I enter a store, I already have in my mind what I need. For example, I need six pairs of black crew socks, a high-quality black leather belt, or a white, short-sleeve shirt with two front pockets. The more details the better. Knowing the price of the item or having a price range makes it easier to save money. Some people love to shop the clearance or sales rack. I always start there—but do you really need a pair of bright orange painter pants that you are never going to wear, buying them just because they're on sale for $9.99? Be careful of clearance or sale rack shopping.

Some people love to go shopping as a form of entertainment. They always go to look but inevitably buy something. If you have a weakness for fashion, a flare for fine shoes, or a romance with rock and roll music, admit it. If it really makes you happy to spend money on your passions, do not eliminate them. Budget a monthly allowance for your passion and stick to it.

Imagine the satisfaction of purchasing an item that you really wanted and could not find for a very long time, such as that special item that completes your much-loved collection of antique telephone poles, or whatever you collect. But here, you purchased that exact hard-to-find item you wanted at 30 percent off. You also paid for it with your allocated or saved money and not a credit card... let it sink in...

Financial happiness is about you controlling your money, and not your money controlling you. Imagine having the money to help someone you truly love without the stress of taking on debt to help him or her. Picture having the money to paint your home or replace the tires of your car without worrying where the money is coming from. Planning allows you to do just that. It takes time, effort, and discipline. The satisfaction is great.

I have always been an impulsive shopper. I am the guy who, walking into a burger joint and seeing the giant-sized posters, buys the special California Avocado Burger with Blue Cheese when I see the advertising. I am a sucker for good advertising: I know it, my family knows it, my friends know it, and I avoid going alone to get burgers.

I am also terrified to enter big box wholesale club stores. Why? Everything is such a good deal. I always wind up buying ten pounds of different cheeses, three pounds of premium olives, a few pounds of prosciutto ham, and exotic foods that drive me crazy. I know I do not need the extra calories or to spend $300 on fancy foods, so I just avoid them like the plague.

If you are in financial trouble due to an addiction or a gambling problem, now is the time to accept it and get help. My humble book is not going to solve your addiction. I pray that you get help and continue on the path toward financial happiness. Life's problems, when taken by the horn and dealt with, provide a great sense of joy, freedom, and happiness.

Local religious institutions are a great source of information and help. If you happen to be a member of a parish, congregation, temple, mosque, or synagogue, call them. You will be surprised at how many people are passionate about helping and the programs available.

Addictions happen in the process to fill an unmet need. I hope you find something truly beautiful to replace your addiction. I know it's out there, but you need to search for it.

After you find help, my book will be waiting for you to continue your journey to financial happiness.

Reflections

Reflections

CHAPTER 6

WAYS TO SAVE

People save money in many different ways. The most important part of the program is finding a system that works for you. I will detail a few common ways people organize their savings. Large or small, the most important factor in selecting a system is that you feel comfortable with it and use it. Savings is a learned behavior. The more you practice, the better you get.

Savings as a concept is quite simple: you put away a small part of everything you make. If you are buying a TV for $500 and have saved for it over the past three months, and then you get a 10 percent off coupon on the day of the sale, it's extra money you were not counting on. *Save it* if you can.

Just a note on discount coupons and promotions: if a retailer that you support produces a discount coupon, use it. Seek out discount coupons, especially on major purchases and big-ticket items. A little pre-purchase research on the web, in newspapers, flyers, or correspondence goes a long way to save you money. An informed consumer is a smart consumer.

I've always heard the saying, "A penny saved is a penny earned." These days, a dollar saved is worth more than a dollar earned; a saved dollar is always after taxes. A $5,000 commission check is worth less than $5,000 in your savings account. Taxes have to yet be paid on the commission check. The higher your tax rate, the higher the worth of your saved dollars.

Taxes on savings and tax-deferred savings vehicles are beyond the scope of this book. IRAs, 401(k)s, annuities, pensions, and deferred compensation plans might be available to you on your path to financial happiness. Your tax adviser or investment adviser will be able to assist you in selecting the best vehicles for you. My advice is to save everywhere you can. Diversify your savings as they grow, and never put all your eggs in one basket. Once you have set up a basic savings program, you will find countless options on financial products that are long term in nature and offer tax deferments. These products also require extra study and shopping. Many of these products and services are sold, not purchased. Many complicated financial products and services are sold by individuals that have specialized training and skills. Regular consumers often do not understand their own purchases. Understand what you are putting your hard-earned money into: you must know the costs, expenses, and penalties associated with the purchase.

Here are a few places you can keep your money.

1) You can simply stuff money into the piggybank, jar, or coffee can until it is full. If you need your money, open the container. I clearly remember a wooden box my father made when I was a child. It was fifteen by fifteen by nine inches. He made it using wood, glue, and nails, and he painted it the same brown as the wooden floor it sat on. He would only put in dimes, quarters, fifty-cent pieces, and dollar coins. When the box was opened years later, it contained almost $2,000. That was a lot of money in the late 1970s. I remember counting and rolling the coins to take to the bank, and it took days to finish. My father's attitude toward his hoard was that it was almost found money. The money had trickled in little by little, and he never felt the sacrifice of saving.

2) The hidden stash of bills, money in the mattress, the stuffed old shoe, the hollowed-out book, the stash under the loose floorboard, the fake electrical socket safe, and so on. People have been hiding money in their homes since money was invented. The only issue that I have with this concept is that the funds are at risk of being lost to fires, storms, criminals, loss of memory, or family members with uncontrollable needs. Be careful and be prudent; if you have too much, put it in a bank or two.

3) You can use a traditional savings account, the most boring of all financial instruments.

4) As your savings increase, there are an infinite number of choices of financial instruments and accounts. The trick is to just get started saving money and accumulating assets.

I was a banker for many years. I always enjoyed dealing with large sums of money, leverages, and rates of return, and I never paid much attention to the savings account. Savings accounts were just boring and simple. After losing all my assets and starting over again, opening a simple $300 savings account gave me tremendous satisfaction. Opening that account showed me that I had started on the path to my financial happiness. A simple saving account is a great starting point. Open one or a few as soon as you can; just stay away from high fees or unrealistic minimum balances. I mention the use of several savings accounts as a form of segregation of assets. The actual earnings from interest will be insignificant. Just put money away.

Yes, I had suffered a loss of career. My assets were consumed. I was working, but at a much lower income level. The lifestyle I had become accustomed to was falling apart in front of my eyes. During this time of financial despair, people also struggling financially started turning to me for advice. I was broke, yet people were asking me for advice. I found it ironic and comical. My family, my training, and my faith was all I had left. I know now how much I had. I struggled to make sense of my life and the economy. I searched for a better-paying job and more income, but it just was not happening.

It took a long time, but I finally accepted my situation, my limited income, and my near-poverty. All I wanted was to be happy again. I wanted to lose my guilt, my shame, and my frustrations of losing the standard of living I was accustomed to. I had to forgive myself and all the people I had blamed for my predicament. That was the turning point in my life. Once I forgave myself, each day I was richer—not by a lot, but I was richer day by day. I was on the path to my financial happiness. I could see the light at the end of the tunnel, and my income would eventually improve. All I had to do was live within my means, stay out of debt, and save all that I could. This is the simple foundation to my financial happiness.

The Three-Legged Stool

Burn the following into your mind; they are the foundation of this book.

The basics to a long-term successful personal budget are simple: 1) live within or below your means; 2) reduce your debt or severely limit credit card use; and 3) maintain regular savings.

Notes

Notes

Your net worth is your accumulated assets minus your debts. The best way to become wealthy is to constantly increase your income, reduce the percentage of expenses as your income increases, and invest your savings in productive endeavors that generate additional growth and income with low risk of loss.

The logic is simple. The execution is the hard part. We are surrounded by beautiful things that are always enticing us to spend money.

CHAPTER 7

BE FRUGAL WHEN SHOPPING

*Don't save what is left after spending; spend what
is left after saving.*—Warren Buffett

I repeat this Buffett quote in the book; I want it to sink in.

Here are a few questions you should ask before purchasing something.

- Am I buying the items for myself or to please someone else?
- Will the item be less expensive in a few weeks?
- Can I wait until I pay for it in cash and avoid using credit?
- What benefits do I get from this purchase?
- Can I substitute something less expensive for this purchase?
- Can the cost be shared?
- Is the item a need or a want?
- Will the item or service only be used in the short term? Is renting or leasing an option?
- Can the money be spent in a better or more productive way?
- Can it be purchased used/second hand?
- Do I really need it?

A good solid budget allows for regular savings, planned purchases, and discretionary purchases of needs and wants.

Let us say your passion is playing basketball, and all you truly want is a pair of special basketball shoes that sell for $250.00. The purchase of the shoes itself can become a catalyst for savings and planning. I might never spend so much on a pair of shoes, but who am I to say that what you are doing is wrong? I think that if you want something and make the effort, you should be able to get it. I want you to remember that everything you see cannot be the item that you want or will die without. Discipline is the key.

Know yourself, your budget, your expectation, your long- and short-term goals, and the true income that you are expecting to earn.

I have always wanted a fancy, expensive sports car. I would really like to have something exotic and fast. The purchase of that vehicle would also have consequences: financial strain on my budget, funds diverted from my family and household, and our savings. The purchase would also create additional costs of maintenance, fuel, and insurance. I am not even taking into account the additional trouble that a sports car could get me into.

A budget is destroyed when an extreme luxury item consumes a large part of the budget.

Everyone has a budget. You might not think so. It might not be formalized. You might have never even thought you had one, but everyone has a budget.

The concept of planning your budget is the part that many have trouble with. This is a learned behavior, and you will be able to do it by the end of this book. You can take control of your budget.

CHAPTER 8

SICK BUDGETS, DEAD BUDGETS

Have you or a friend ever attempted to pay for groceries and the clerk informs you that your card has been declined? Remember "the budget you did not know you had screaming for help" mentioned earlier in the book? That budget was sick and needed help.

Sleepless nights, family arguments, and fights over money are also signs that a budget is quickly in need of help.

Radical advice: if you find that your budget and finances are out of control or in a death spiral, just stop! Close your bank accounts and open new ones. Cut up your credit cards and only use cash. Is your credit rating destroyed? Are your credit cards tapped out? Are you constantly paying over-the-limit fees on your credit cards? Are you several months behind on your mortgage? Are you paying several overdraft fees every month on your bank account? Just stop!

Do you know someone who has had to file for bankruptcy? That was a budget that had simply died and was laid to rest. That person is not without a budget, though. As soon as a person is discharged from bankruptcy, a new budget is born. A new budget needs to be nurtured. These new post-bankruptcy budgets or plans require a lot of effort. Just like a newborn baby, a lot of dirty diapers will have to be changed along with much cleaning. Many first steps will also have to be taken.

A new post-bankruptcy budget is a wonderful thing. The debts that killed the old budget are mostly gone. The new focus is to increase incomes, continue reducing expenses, and aggressively saving money.

I tell people that post-bankruptcy budgets are the same as those of a high school graduate or a newly arrived immigrant: little or no debt, no assets, no credit, and little income. The idea is simply to create assets, incomes, and savings. Concentrating on creating a realistic plan and budget is crucial.

You might have passed the point of no return and need to contemplate bankruptcy. Seek an attorney and review your options. On the other hand, if the amount you owe on your total credit is small and the cause of your financial woes is mismanagement, a few weeks of financial non-activity might reset your finances. Be very careful!

I'm not suggesting you just stop paying your bills. It's a "hard reset," like when a battery is removed from a laptop. You wait a little while and insert the battery to resume working on it again. As in the case of the laptop, be careful to do things right.

"Financial fasting" is a budgetary concept that is seldom spoken about. Have you ever tried to go shopping and you left your wallet at home? You probably did not spend much money on that trip to the mall. Keep it simple. Start on your day off or on a weekend, leave your debit cards, and credit cards at home, and see how much money you spend. Concentrate on prepaid, free or low cost activities. Only take minimal amounts of cash. At first it will be a little strange; you'll basically feel naked. Eventually you will become accustomed to walking around without cash, debit cards, and credit cards.

You spend more money on your days off than when you are working. Why? You have the time to go shopping. Try financial fasting for a few days. It is very simple. Just do not spend any money. The day after the financial fasting, do not rush out to the stores and spend all the money you saved. Again be very careful think about what you are trying to achieve—financial happiness.

During your first days of financial fasting you might want to go out and spend. If you are just bored or have no one to call or visit, take a detailed inventory of everything you have. Count socks, shirts, underwear, screws, pots, pans, and soap bars. Write it down. You will be amazed at how much stuff you have and the cost (value) of it all. If you have eighty-two pairs of size twenty-eight jeans from your high school days and realistically feel you are never going to wear them again, do something with them. Sell them, give them away, or donate them; you might not be able to use them, but they might be used by someone who has less than you.

Inventory is the list of items a business has to sell. In Miami, my hometown, used clothing has become more than a business, it has become an industry. If you have eighty-two pairs of vintage jeans, they have a value. They can be sold at a yard sale, a flea market, even placed in a consignment shop. We in Miami sell vintage stoves, vintage furniture, vintage clothes, even vintage vacations, vintage cars, and vintage boats. We have large and small thrift shops. I have noticed the value of the same item change as it goes from trash to unwanted, to unneeded, to used, to retro, to vintage, to collectable, to antique. It's the same item. All that changes is the presentation and price. Bottom line, clean up your clutter and do something with it.

CHAPTER 9

FRUGALITY

The body size and shape of a long-distance runner and a Sumo wrestler are extremely different. The sports these athletes practice require different attributes and skills. A long-distance runner needs speed and lightness of body to allow for swiftness and stamina. A Sumo wrestler needs power and the ability to resist a large amount of weight that is charging him, and his large mass is an asset.

Why am I writing about sports and finances? Simply that an athlete needs to concentrate on training and seek attributes that will help him or her win in his or her selected sport. In a household budget, you also need to concentrate only on attributes that help you succeed. Saving money on everyday items and services is a factor that contributes to your ability to save money.

Being frugal is more than just saving money. Frugality is really about squeezing every usable drop out of every liquid, product, item, or service you use.

Becoming a smart shopper is a great way to improve your finances. If you are going to buy twenty gallons of gasoline every week, why not save three cents a gallon by pumping gas on Wednesdays (discount day) and using your grocery rewards discount at the same time? A typical savings with gasoline at four dollars a gallon is twenty-three cents times twenty gallons, which come to $4.60, plus 2 percent cash back on $80 is $1.60, which now totals $6.20. In my house, that translates to a gallon of milk and a loaf of bread. This small change in how I shop for gasoline becomes more than $300 saved per year.

The math is simple: $6.20 x 52 weeks = $317.20. This amount is greater than the amount that I opened my savings account with.

You Can Fill a Bucket One Drop at a Time

Many savings habits are very simple. The more you practice them, the better you get. Lots of books have been written on this subject, and a quick Internet search will give you hundreds of ideas.

Over the pasts few years the concept of couponing has gained popularity. When the economy starts to constrict, people look for solutions to buy the things they need. In this last recession, rising commodity prices placed additional pressures on the budgets of those already struggling. A dozen coupons a week can easily add $10 to $20 to your family's food budget. Together with taking advantage of in-store specials, BOGOs (buy-one, get-one free), and avoiding excessive premium products, a family can reduce their budget without drastically changing their diets. A simple tip: never shop for groceries while hungry.

Companies invest in coupons as a way to get the consumer to buy their goods. Do not fall into the trap on buying items that are not going to be used simply because you have a coupon. Also, expensive snacks, fatty junk foods, and highly processed foods might not necessarily be what you want to buy just because they are cheap.

A healthy meal goes a long way. If you are a good cook, make a little extra to have for lunch a few times a week. One of the simplest ways to save money is to brown bag your lunch.

In my experience, casual dining (moderately priced lunches and dinners) is one of the four largest monthly expenses in budgets that are in disarray. If you are going to eat out, try using coupons or discounts available on your cell phones. By slightly changing your food choices (e.g., substituting water for soft drinks, skipping dessert, or sharing a larger platter), you will be able to still enjoy dining out while saving a few dollars and protecting your waistline. I personally enjoy eating lunch in a restaurant. By slightly shifting spending habits, you can continue any activity the makes you happy.

I want you to understand that this book is about balance. Financial happiness is all about balance. You need to eat every day, so just slightly adjust your habits and bank the savings.

The man known as Buddha—"the Enlightened One"—was born Siddhartha Gautama around the sixth century BC. His father was a king who gave him a life of wealth and royal luxury. He lived in a palace and enjoyed a sheltered life. One day, Siddhartha left his royal residence to discover a world full of suffering and poverty. He left his kingdom to try to find a way to help those who suffered in life. He spent many years studying different methods of meditation with an array of religious teachers.

One day, a girl named Sujata offered him a bowl of rice (in some versions it's milk and rice pudding), and this made him realize that there is more to life than material things and physical discipline. At age thirty-five, Siddhartha achieved enlightenment and became Buddha.

A good balance in your financial life will bring you happiness. I cannot tell you to just save, save, save, and live a life of sacrifice. Financial happiness is a combination of living within your means, regular savings, and low debt. Your struggle to improve your finances will allow you to taste how wonderful a bowl of rice really is. Enjoyment, laughter, beauty, hope, and love are all around us. We just have to be open and able to accept their existence.

Flash Exercise

Try to find another $_____ (aim for $200) of savings in ten regular monthly expenses.

	Expense	Description	Normal Cost	Monthly Savings
1.	_____	_____	_____	_____
2.	_____	_____	_____	_____
3.	_____	_____	_____	_____
4.	_____	_____	_____	_____
5.	_____	_____	_____	_____
6.	_____	_____	_____	_____
7.	_____	_____	_____	_____
8.	_____	_____	_____	_____
9.	_____	_____	_____	_____
10.	_____	_____	_____	_____

Total Savings Found: _____

CHAPTER 10

MATERIAL THINGS

I had spent the day writing about savings, being frugal and deferred gratification. I turned on the TV to relax before going to sleep. The first show that I tuned into was about emeralds and their great value. The show's host was explaining how the value of emerald lies in the power and wealth that they portray. I did not like the concept and changed the channel. The next channel had on a show about multimillion-dollar recreational vehicles. The next channel had on a show about high-end luxury cruises. The next show was about living large in Dubai. I just turned off the TV and went to sleep.

We live in a world that is constantly tempting us to spend money. The advertisers attempt to make us think we can only be happy if we possess their items. This mindset is the basis of aspirational wealth.

Selling $1,000 designer handbags to secretaries who make $18,000 a year is a great marketing ploy. Many of the women buying the bags probably do not have the money in their bank accounts but do have the available credit on a credit card. The sad part is not the purchase of this beautiful and well-made handbag; the high quality will probably last many years. The sad part is that the bag will stop being used long before the credit balance is paid off.

Beautiful clothes and shoes, exquisite perfumes, good food and wine, luxurious travel, finely appointed homes, and of course expensive automobiles are all symbols of wealth. If you can afford them, they represent the good life.

If you cannot afford them, you fall into the trap of aspirational wealth. This could develop into frustration, a sense of envy, and even resentment. The old-fashioned concept of "keeping up with the Joneses" (you can even add "on steroids") is what I refer to as aspirational wealth": "I want this type of car" or "this type of phone" or "this type of lifestyle." Let's just be aware of the concept and be careful of falling too deeply into a desire to possess anything beyond our means.

You shall not covet your neighbor's wife, or his male servant, or his female servant, or his ox, or his donkey, or anything that is your neighbor's.—Exodus 20:17

Material things serve their purpose. Beautiful things inspire and motivate many individuals to work very hard. It is good practice to reward yourself when you hit certain goals. A reward for achieving a goal of saving $500 in four weeks might be a steak dinner, cologne, or a new pair of sneakers.

People in sales often use material things, dollars, and constant accumulation as a way to stay motivated and focused. The ups and downs of a sales position are stressful. The constant rejection, the hang-ups, the lack of belief in what you are selling, the sales goals, and the inconsistent incomes make commission-based jobs difficult. A person with unsteady income has to be focused and potentially work harder to keep his or her finances in order. The ability to save that large commission check and avoid the temptation of spending it as soon as it arrives is foundation stone of financial happiness for a person or family who lives with a variable income.

People in the entertainment or sports industries also face similar pressure. The wealth, fame, and beauty of the careers tend to be short-lived. The glamorous trappings of the industries lead many to addiction and bankruptcy. The focus on youth, beauty, performance, and wealth can take a huge toll on even the most disciplined.

Too many professional athletes who come from humble beginnings lose all their millions in just a few years after their careers end. Financial planning, preparing for a young retirement, savings, and a humble heart should start with the first big paycheck. Most often excessive consumption and living beyond their actual means is the norm, hence no savings or no planning. One injury or personal misjudgment can destroy a career overnight. Many of the great ones stay focused and they plan. They educate themselves, invest large portions of their incomes, and live with the reality that their special careers are short. They know they need to plan, budget, and prepare for the next stage of theirs lives.

A material goal to motivate yourself can be a great source of inspiration. Rewards become markers or reminders that you are on track and moving forward. The trick is not to let the accumulation of material things be the only reason for living. Money is just a tool. Avoid spending money on items and services that you might not really need. Control your money, and never let your money control you.

CHAPTER 11

THE CHECKLIST

Please review the checklist to financial happiness again. It will serves as a guidepost, and the progress tracker will help record your success. None of the goals or items on the checklist is absolute. The goals should be modified as your own. *The Little Green Book of Financial Happiness* was not written with any absolute authority; it's just a guide.

Please review the first financial happiness checklist and get a good feel for how it was set up. The blank spaces for your own goals will play a more important role this time around. The beautiful thing about the program is that you can always change or add goals. As the weeks pass on your path to financial happiness, you will start seeing things differently. This book's purpose is to improve your overall financial well-being.

A good exercise is to review your first cash-flow and first net-worth worksheet/balance sheet. After reviewing your balance sheet and cash-flow statement, please turn to the financial happiness progress tracker. Please fill out a new net worth balance sheet and savings worksheet and record the number in the financial happiness progress tracker with today's date. Look hard to see all the improvements you have made so far.

This is a good time to review your financial happiness checklists.

Flash Exercise

Try to find a few new potential sources of income for your future.

Target income desired: _____

This exercise will show you the potential for getting ahead. The mostly humble of us have the ability to earn significantly more than we are currently earning. These new sources of income can be dedicated to a specific goal: buying a home, saving for retirement, sending a child to college. Take your time and think about it. If you believe in prayer or meditation, this is a good time to put your beliefs into practice.

Some options are selling homemade honey or firewood, working part-time at the local zoo, fixing vintage radios, or whatever. Just think! If you cannot do this exercise now, think about it for a few days or weeks, but do it.

Check List Notes

Check List Notes

CHAPTER 12

THE CLASS THAT MORPHED INTO THIS BOOK

I have conducted this class in a church group setting for more than ten years. The class was called Financial Survival Workshop. It was designed to help people who were struggling with their finances due to job loss, reduced income, and the real estate crisis. As the years passed, I started to notice people becoming sad, frustrated, and even suicidal about their budgets. I knew at that point I was not doing enough. I was only dealing with the finance issues as a mathematical exercise. The problems were emotional and I was unprepared to help.

I was now also struggling financially myself and had no one to turn to for help. I am well educated and have a deep knowledge base of finances, banking, and economics. I just did not have enough income to maintain my lifestyle. I was feeling that my party was over, and I just wanted to be happy again. I had always been happy-go-lucky, never took anything too, too serious, or really cared about showing off my wealth. I was just struggling due to lack of income; I had consumed my savings and was not seeing many opportunities on the horizon. In the middle of all my personal turmoil, people I knew started to call me for advice.

Everyone had the same problems: lack of income, too much debt, and depleted savings. We were all broke and miserable. It is hard to lose everything you had and have to start over from zero. I started seeking help from friends who had solid spiritual foundations, the clergy, and a few psychologists. I shared my dilemma and told them I was not trained to deal with emotional issues. They all told me they were not trained to deal with money issues. They told me to listen respectfully, to not judge people, and to guide them as best as I could. I then started months of reading about a variety of emotional and psychological subjects. I came to a simple conclusion. All the issues could be resolved if people forgave the causes of their problems and themselves, regained the hope that life would eventually improve, and recognized that love and happiness are free.

Notes and Comments

Notes and Comments

A good friend, a powerful man in his early fifties, was crying while he told me his financial woes. He was pouring out his soul to me, and I had no preparation to deal with this situation. After I listened to him for twenty minutes and he regained his composure, he then asked me what I thought and to give him an answer. My head was still spinning as I said, "It is true, you are broke. You and your family have your health and faith still intact. On the other hand, your bank has a very serious problem—you owe them $1,250,000 and your house is going to barely sell for $500,000 in a foreclosure auction. Your bank is the one that should be crying, not you. You just need to speak to a bankruptcy attorney and get a new job."

Imagine a sixteen-ounce glass of water with eight ounces in it. The glass of water can be seen as half-empty, half-full, or for having the potential to quench your thirst.

The beautiful part of being at zero is that you really cannot lose any more. If you feel you still have more to lose, then you are not really at zero.

Ponder this idea: you have a true overabundance of faith, joy, hope, and happiness. Do you really need material things? Would you honestly trade the overabundance of faith, joy, hope, and happiness for $10 million?

In all cultures around the world, people laugh and smile no matter how rich or poor.

CHAPTER 13

CREATING WEALTH

We need to create plenty of meaningful jobs. Good jobs allow people to feel useful, productive, and progressive. When a business creates a product or a service that becomes important or in high demand, it creates meaningful jobs. They provide growth of income, upward mobility, and interest in working for such a business. We as a people search for continuous growth and stability.

Wealth is created when we mine, grow, catch, make, or sell a product or a service that generates a net profit. For example, when we mine gold with a cost of $1,000 an ounce and sell the finished product at $1,600 an ounce, it makes a $600 profit. We create wealth at a number of different levels. First income and profits come to the company that sells the machines and equipment to operate the mine. The basic utilities and the providers of basic commodities used in the process also generate sales and profits. The workers and operators of the mine receive a share in the form of wages and salaries, and shareholders of the companies receive the residual profits. The business people hopefully profit from trading gold. Countries also benefit in the form of taxes and duties that they receive from companies and their suppliers, as well as the taxes paid by the employees who work in the mine.

The economy of the gold mining area also experiences a multiplying effect of wealth as people spend, save, and invest the moneys generated. The effect is called the velocity of money. Every dollar spent is recycled several times throughout the economy. This is a classic description of an economy in expansion mode.

Flash Exercise

Try to find a few new potential sources of income for your future.

Before you start, review the first flash exercise you did in Chapter 11.

Target extra income desired: $_____

This exercise is to illustrate the potential for getting ahead. Again, the mostly humble of us have the ability to earn significantly more than we are currently earning. These new sources of income can be dedicated to a specific goal: buying a home, saving for retirement, sending a child to college, etc. Take your time and think about it. If you believe in prayer or meditation, this is a good time to put your beliefs into practice.

Think of other different things to do—recycling, selling stuff you do not need, selling your widget collection on eBay for a profit—that could allow you to continue expanding your collection or passion.

	Description	Monthly Earnings	Annual Potential
1.	_____	_____	_____
2.	_____	_____	_____
3.	_____	_____	_____
4.	_____	_____	_____
5.	_____	_____	_____
6.	_____	_____	_____
7.	_____	_____	_____
8.	_____	_____	_____
9.	_____	_____	_____
10.	_____	_____	_____

What Can I Do to Make Money?

What Can I Do to Make Money?

Financial Happiness Monthly Progress Tracker

This will demonstrate your progress toward financial happiness.

Date _____ / _____ / _____

_____ month #_____

1. Net worth (today) $_____
2. Total cash (today) $_____
3. Total debt (today) $_____
4. Total income (this month) $_____
5. Amount saved (this month) $_____
6. What goals did you accomplish this month? _____
   _____
   _____
   _____

Financial Happiness Monthly Progress Tracker

This will demonstrate your progress toward financial happiness.

Date _____ / _____ / _____

_____ month #_____

1. Net worth (today) $_____
2. Total cash (today) $_____
3. Total debt (today) $_____
4. Total income (this month) $_____
5. Amount saved (this month) $_____
6. What goals did you accomplish this month? _____
   _____
   _____
   _____

Financial Happiness Monthly Progress Tracker

This will demonstrate your progress toward financial happiness.

Date _____ / _____ / _____

_____ month #_____

1. Net worth (today) $_____
2. Total cash (today) $_____
3. Total debt (today) $_____
4. Total income (this month) $_____
5. Amount saved (this month) $_____
6. What goals did you accomplish this month? _____
   _____
   _____
   _____

Financial Happiness Monthly Progress Tracker

This will demonstrate your progress toward financial happiness.

Date _____ / _____ / _____

_____ month #_____

1. Net worth (today) $_____
2. Total cash (today) $_____
3. Total debt (today) $_____
4. Total income (this month) $_____
5. Amount saved (this month) $_____
6. What goals did you accomplish this month? _____
   _____
   _____
   _____

Financial Happiness Monthly Progress Tracker

This will demonstrate your progress toward financial happiness.

Date _____ / _____ / _____

_____ month #_____

1. Net worth (today) $_____
2. Total cash (today) $_____
3. Total debt (today) $_____
4. Total income (this month) $_____
5. Amount saved (this month) $_____
6. What goals did you accomplish this month? _____
   _____
   _____
   _____

Financial Happiness Monthly Progress Tracker

This will demonstrate your progress toward financial happiness.

Date _____ / _____ / _____

_____ month #_____

1. Net worth (today) $_____
2. Total cash (today) $_____
3. Total debt (today) $_____
4. Total income (this month) $_____
5. Amount saved (this month) $_____
6. What goals did you accomplish this month? _____
   _____
   _____
   _____

CHAPTER 14

A FEW SIMPLIFIED SCENARIOS

Following are a few scenarios illustrating how a few simple changes improved people's finances. I engaged with these people during the class and through my years providing guidance before this book was written.

A—A family was struggling to make ends meet. We ran numbers, and the family had a deficit of $800 a month. Their house was on the line/danger, but they could no longer get their mortgage refinanced or a take out a line of credit. The wife was not working. They had no savings left and credit cards at their maximum with more than $400 in monthly payments. The credit scores were damaged due to late payments. Bankruptcy for this family was not an option due to minimal debt. Solutions were to cut expenses, cut back credit card payments or get on a payment plan with credit card companies, and for the wife to get a part-time job. A few months later a better-paying job for the husband became available and helped rebalance the new budget. A savings program was established shortly after.

B—A married couple owed more on their home than it was currently worth, had too much credit card debt, no saving, home in foreclosure, significant drop in family income, and large pension from previous job. Solution: they consulted an attorney and filed bankruptcy. The family was able to protect a large 401(k) and eventually moved to a rental home. They started a saving program. The husband is looking for more income or a better job. Family is dreaming again of one day buying a humble home.

C—A divorced and single woman was renting a high-end apartment, had no savings left, lost her job, and had a lot of credit card debt. Solution: took a lower-paying job (because she could not get a better job) and rented a cheaper apartment and moved forward. She negotiated with credit card companies through a credit consulting service and received a major reduction on total debt and payments. She has a new part-time job and started a savings program. This person just accepted to live within her means.

D—A very successful businessman, married with large family. His income was dramatically reduced. Credit card debt was in the six-figure range. He had several properties that were upside down and in short sale process. Home was short sold. A short sale is the process where a bank accepts less for the debt on a home owed to it, to quicken the foreclosure process and takes possession of the property from the homeowner that defaulted on the mortgage or equity line.

He was pushing himself to the point of a nervous breakdown. I knew he was struggling financially, but he had a very good prospect to increase income in the future. Bankruptcy was not carried out after attorney reviewed his situation. The family had too many assets. Solution: he finally accepted his financial situation and reduction in income. The family drastically reduced expenses, eliminated expensive hobbies, and sold off a few assets, which allowed him to get his household under control. The expensive boat was sold at a small loss. Wife went back to work. The family rented a home to accommodate kids until they finished college and moved on. Family started to plan and save for retirement with a humble heart and an open mind.

Everyone is different, with different needs, problems, opportunities, and situations. A little discipline, hard work, faith, and truly understanding your budget can lead you to a better financial reality and financial happiness.

CHAPTER 15

THE STORY BEHIND THIS BOOK

On August 28, 2008, I was having a great time in my friend Paul's pool. I had been drinking large amounts of expensive rum while eating and playing with all the kids in the pool. I had a great buzz, was acting like a big kid in the pool, and all the adults at the party were just having a great old time. Then I received a call from a coworker, Billy. I knew something was wrong since Billy never called me on my cell phone on a Sunday. He told me to turn on the business news. The bank I worked for was being purchased by another bank for very little per share! I knew I had just lost a small fortune in my 401(k), probably my career, and definitely the great buzz I was feeling.

As the months passed, the stress of my financial burdens became apparent to me. My standard of living was quickly declining before my eyes, and I had no idea how to change it. Everyone was telling me to just relax, but I was not only dealing with my own problems, I was handling countless clients going through similar situations. It started to negatively affect me. I was not sleeping, was constantly upset at home, and I could not relax. Two years after the merger I left the bank, since I felt that I could no longer function giving financial advice. My personal financial situation and my opinions of what was going on in the economy were at odds with what I felt my employer was advocating. I felt lost; my father had passed away, and I truly did not know to who to turn to for help or advice. I was the financial adviser and had no idea what to do.

Over the next two years, I suffered and survived a major financial setback. The current economic situation has had a major negative impact on my career as a banker and on my personal finances. I was working selling logistics services and making much less than I was accustomed to. My situation pushed me to the brink of sorrow, depression, and hopelessness. I was only kept afloat by my faith and the love of my family and friends.

My financial training, education, and the countless phone calls from people also struggling allowed my mind to become calm.

In my own financial distress, I have found myself guiding people who had sought my advice. At first, I found it ironic. *People asking* me *for advice,* I would think. I would run a simple cash-flow analysis with them, giving basic guidance, and quickly find the deficit and budget accordingly. I found that many of the people I was helping were truly grateful and a lot more relaxed after our meeting. My own experience became transitory and almost a source of solace.

My wife and I basically agreed that if the family stayed together and were healthy, how we lived was not important. We recognized that we were poorer than how we felt. We were very disappointed, but it finally allowed us to start moving forward. We started budgeting, cutting corners, planning, reducing the rates of our services/utilities, and eliminating expenses everywhere we could. The concept we live with now is, if we do not have the cash, we wait or do not buy it.

Most importantly, we started saving again. It was very modest. I went to open a savings account with $300 and felt a huge amount of satisfaction. I was starting to see something positive amongst all the negativity.

I then continued guiding whomever I could. As the years passed, my wife and I continued saving, living within our means, and not taking on debt.

I am still working at the same logistics company, only with the possibility of additional large projects slowly coming onboard. I do consulting work on the side and teach finance at the local college. I still occasionally teach sessions at my church whenever I am asked. Now the class is called financial happiness instead of financial survival.

CHAPTER 16

WHAT HAPPENED TO OUR ECONOMY?

The economy and what happened, in my humble opinion, is that the tech bubble exploded in 2000 and the financial markets fell into disarray. The US Federal Reserve eased interest rates to accommodate the recession. They wanted to create growth in the economy.

On September 11, 2001, the United States was attacked by terrorists. No one saw it coming. The attacks resulted in the different wars in the Middle East and a lot more easing by the Federal Reserve to again create some growth in the economy.

All the easing or reduction of interest rates caused the largest expansion of commodity, financial asset and real estate prices ever seen. Home prices rose at a very fast pace, induced by easy credit, speculation, and greed.

From 2000 to 2007 the banks were lending with both hands. Many people were using the newly created equity of their homes to expand their standards of living. People felt wealthier, were eating out more often, and repairing their homes with better fixtures, taking vacations, starting businesses, buying additional real estate since "property values always go up." This was the classic real estate bubble.

In 2007 the real estate bubble started to pop. Banks stopped lending, prices started declining, people started to simply walk away from secondary homes. The majority of these homes had been recently purchased or refinanced at very high loan-to-value ratios. They could not sell or rent them at a rate high enough to cover their costs. The pain in the economy started to become apparent, especially in Miami. My home town, Miami, was at the epic center of the housing boom. The types of homes built, the high values of the properties, the very high loans to values of the properties and the sporadic nature of the local incomes.

Five years later and the pains from the real estate crisis are still not over. In Miami, in my primitive opinion, prices will continue falling for many years. The banks are full of the so-called shadow inventory. Shadow inventory is an unknown or undisclosed number of homes that banks have not foreclosed on, but that their loans are in default and qualify to be foreclosed on. The banks are just waiting for as long as they can. Lending standards are high and financing of current homes is limited. We will be in this mess for a long time. The brightest spot on the local real estate horizon in south Florida is that foreigners and private investors are buying a lot of property. Let's just hope they can hold on to the properties long enough for the economy to bounce back.

Our standard of living shows why the pain is so apparent. The country's standard of living quickly rose in the years following the Clinton era. These increases in our standard of living were basically financed with new debt in the forms of credit cards, mortgages, and home equity lines. The houses that were built were bigger, better, fancier, and more expensive to maintain. Many homes had amenities such as spas, pools, fancy yards, cabanas, etc. The same thing happened to our cars, our eating habits, and even our entertainment.

The reduced incomes were caused by losses of jobs, reductions of commissions, reductions of pay, and closure of credit lines.

What happens when the budget to finance our standard of living drops dramatically? Bad things happen: *pain, despair, confusion, stress, anger, fear,* and *envy*.

This is the *financial hangover*; like a chemically induced hangover it is slow to be recognized and even slower to be acted upon. This financial hangover is like a train that you are on, just in slow motion. You do not jump off the train but instead ball up into a fetal position and wait for the impact. You hope and pray that it will go away and things will return to the ways they were—*normal.*

During the year 2007, things were not *normal.* It was just crazy, a cheap money-induced party that was out of control. Almost every business benefited from the expansion. People and businesses that sold homes, cars, bread, tiles, airplanes, boats, horses, services, even charities and religious institution all benefited. The money was just flowing.

The party is now over; this is the hangover.

I personally hate the term the "new normal." We're experiencing slow growth, a high unemployment rate, and the reduction en mass of standards of living. People are affected in different ways by this changing economy. The standard of living of a family is determined using their income or cash flow. This cash flow will basically decide how well that family will live.

The amount of sorrow and pain that is being experienced by people struggling financially is very great. The recession has not just thinned the wallets of the general population but has shaken their core beliefs. The global marketplace has placed untold pressures on companies and American families to cut costs and grow lean. New technologies are replacing many basic jobs. The middle-aged and middle class are probably the most affected. This is causing a general reduction of our expected standard of living, which is simply controlled by a financial budget.

The recognition of the changes in the family's budget and implementing a new strategy can bring peace and hope to struggling families. A calm mind can get back to work and start enjoying life again.

The pain is caused by changes in their standards of living. This pain comes to people and families that have taken on a lot of debt. The debt cannot be eliminated, reduced, or canceled by quickly selling off or renting the assets. Why? The prices of the underlying collateral are falling quickly, and financing is limited.

CHAPTER 17

ARE YOU BROKE?
YOU STILL HAVE OPTIONS

Seeking credit counseling or bankruptcy, falling delinquent on your debts, negotiating with banks, experiencing short sales, and leaving the country are all options. You always have options. Even doing nothing is an option.

Before we speak about money, let us define "crazy": "Doing the same thing over and over while expecting different results."

Let's talk about money and being broke.

If you owe $20.00 to your bank and you have no money in your account, you have a problem. The bank will overdraw your account and charge you an insufficient funds fee. You must pay back the moneys owed on time to the bank or they will close your account and charge you an account closure fee. Lack of timely payment will make the bank write off your closed account and possibly report you to Chex System.

This might render you an un-bankable individual.

If you owe the bank $20 million on a building that is now worth $5 million and you do not have money in your account, the bank has a problem. Everything is relative. Everything is also negotiable.

If you are doing just fine, you might need to just "toughen up." The pains and fears are still very real. Just adjust your budget, change a few habits, and sprinkle a little frugality into your way of life.

If you are well off or have legal or tax questions, I request that you contact a professional in the specific area of your needs. I also would like to remind you that donations are tax deductible. Please help others if you can. You will find a lot of happiness and joy in sharing your wealth.

Thoughts on life with less Debt

Thoughts on life with less Debt

CHAPTER 18

DEBT

Debt is money owed and an agreement to pay for property, goods, or services rendered. Large credit card balance, large monthly payments, and high debt levels are extremely dangerous. Debt can be a wonderful thing during times of expansion and/or stable economic conditions. In times of falling revenues, economic collapse, or high unemployment it can be a difficult situation to deal with.

The high numbers of personal bankruptcy in our current economy are a function of high debt levels, falling real estate values, lack of credit, and reduced incomes. The media and politicians often speak of fraud and speculation as the causes of our current economic woes. As incomes fell and asset prices start adjusting, people, companies, and governments with high levels of debt started feeling a lot of pain. Fraud and speculation were a small part of a greater problem.

The study of finance has a large set of simple and extremely helpful calculations. These calculations are referred to as ratios. These ratios allow for quick guidance and focus on different areas of a budget analysis. Ratios convert raw numbers or dollars into a proportional system that allows for quick comparisons even amongst radically different budgets.

We will review and work with three commonly used ratios: loan-to-value ratio, debt-to-income ratio, and reserve (cash on hand) ratio.

Loan-to-Value Ratio

Current loan amount/market value of asset =

Conventional or traditional home financing was an 80 percent loan-to-value loan. The 20 percent down payment was created a cushion of protection as home prices fell. What happens when that cushion disappears?

Most of these traditional loans have a fixed interest rate and a specific number of payments. As time passed, the loan balance would shrink, and the equity position would improve for both the homeowner and the bank.

In the past forty years, the US government designed programs to increase home ownership amongst the masses and helped reduce down payment requirements.

The following are a few examples of mortgages that were available in the market:

- Ten percent down payment programs;
- Three-and-a-half percent down payment FHA first-time homebuyer programs;
- No-money-down, GI Bill loans for military personnel;
- The infamous "ninja loan" (no income, no job, no assets); all that supported the loan was the applicant credit rating and the "value" of the collateral; and
- Eighty/twenty mortgages (with an 80 percent down payment first mortgage with a 20 percent piggyback second mortgage). These loans became the standards in many markets and had zero equity cushions. The borrower only had at risk their credit rating and any fees paid at closing.

All the previously discussed mortgages were a wonderful set of programs in a growing and expanding economy, especially with increased home prices, but a nightmare scenario in tough times.

Going back to loan-to-value ratios, once the loan-to-value ratio approaches or surpasses one (1), default rates start to dramatically rise. This is the definition of an "underwater asset". An underwater asset or underwater home is a property that owes more on that it is worth. In the Financial Happiness Workshops I always say "SCUBA SFL would help you breathe if your home was underwater".

For example, a house is purchased for $300,000 with a $20,000 down payment and a loan is issued for $280,000. Two years later the owner of the home loses his or her job. The homeowner attempts to sell the home, but it is now only worth $200,000. The house and loan are both underwater, and trouble is at hand. The bank does not have enough value to cover the loan amount in case of a default, and the homeowner cannot sell off the property to cover the debt and downsize. The equity cushion disappeared for both the homeowner and the bank. This is the situation much of the economy is currently facing.

An unemployed person with a weak balance sheet or lack of savings has few options. The person needs to quickly replace the income lost or make hard decisions about his or her finances. Bankruptcy, credit counseling, short sales, and deed in lieu become some of the few available options. All are hard choices caused by unsustainable debt levels, weak reserves, poor lending practices, and a sluggish economy.

In previous economic downturns, people who lost employment were normally able to downsize quickly, sell their home, and take the equity they had left to start a saving program for their next home. They expected to return to a more normal earning situation, and the job lost was consider a transitional period.

The current economy does not offer the same mobility or opportunity for adjustment of household budgets. Dealing with debt is the last thing anyone needs during a loss of employment or loss of a business.

Debt-to-income ratio is

Total monthly debt payments/monthly income

For example, $1,300 total monthly payments/$2,900
monthly income = 44.8275 percent

During normal economic times, people with stable jobs and careers would take debt at ever-higher percentages of their total income. With low interest rates (percent fixed for a thirty-year mortgage), a person could purchase a home with a $300,000 mortgage loan for $1,800 plus taxes and insurance. At the writing of this book, the thirty-year fixed mortgages rates are lower than 4 percent (historically very low). That is a lot of house for $1,800 a month. What happens if the homeowner's good job disappears and the homeowner cannot replace the income or sell his home? Pain, lots and lots of pain, sleepless nights, frustration, fear, hopelessness, and dispair happens.

When total debt payment rises close to 100 percent of income, very little money is left for saving or even to eat and pay for living expenses. As debt level increases, regular savings become harder. As you approach 100% of total income, debt starts to accumulate on debt. All your income is dedicated to just servicing your debt. This can only be maintained for short periods. If income regularly goes up and down, then debt has to be reduced significantly when funds arrive.

Excessive debt loads can create a so-called "death spiral." Where everything you make goes to pay your creditors, terms on your debt become harsher and defaults of loans are just a few steps away. Your income can stop and be reduced for any of the following reasons—loss of job, reduction of income, destructive weather and "acts of God," acts of war, health issues, or a change in family structure. Any of these can destroy a budget with high debt levels.

Avoid excessive debt! Financial happiness comes from knowing when to avoid or resist taking on too much debt.

Remember: "The rich rule over the poor, and the borrower is slave to the lender". (Proverbs 22:7).

Reserve (cash on hand) ratio

Total cash in saving (including investments)/monthly expenses = Reserve or cash on hand

For example: $11,400/$2,700 = 4.22 months of reserves

Ratios are basic mathematical benchmarks. They are objective and cold. Cuts in budgets, forced savings, eliminating items from our diets, forgoing pleasures, living frugally, and abstaining from wants are hard to deal with and are subjective in nature.

Subjective decisions are normally done with the heart, not the mind. Most budgeting programs discuss and preach about cutting expenses, saving money, and living frugally. Most people ignore budgeting altogether to avoid dealing with hard decisions.

Try to always understand your financial situation and the strength of your balance sheet. It does not make sense to purchase something with a lot of credit, especially if you cannot afford it. Common sense is a rare commodity when lust and desires of beautiful things blinds us into becoming indebted for them. Financial happiness is also having the knowledge to avoid buying something that will cause you pain, guilt, economic loss, and sleepless nights.

"Wise men learn by other men's mistakes; fools by their own"

Alfred Adler, 1870-1937, was an Austrian psychiatrist whose influential system of individual psychology introduced the term "inferiority feeling", which was later widely and often inaccurately called "inferiority complex".

I have included two planners that are helpful for mid- and long-term planning. Place effort in this exercise and remember, it can always be changed, adjusted, or eliminated.

Mid-Term Saving Projects:

This list is for targeted savings for pending purchases or expenditures. List all items you are saving for. Mark with a star items that are inherently unavoidable (e g., replace washing machine).

Target Date	Description	Estimated Cost	Date Acquired	Price	Amount Saved

Total saved: $_____

Mark with two stars items that will upset your monthly budget if they occur prematurely (e. g., replace four tires).

Long-term savings projects:

(For example, trip to theme park for five people. Estimated cost $2500. Program of saving: $200/month for twelve months will result in $2,400. Final cost of trip is $2,275.)

Target Date	Description	Estimated Cost	Date Acquired	Price	Amount Saved

Total saved: $_____

If you need to replace your pickup truck's engine in four months at an estimated $1,000, you need to save $250 per month. If you can save $200 on the engine, that is a 20 percent savings. A few phone calls or a little research goes a long way for some purchasers. Crunch a few numbers, and you will start to view things differently. Putting a new engine on a credit card with available balance is easy to do, but paying for the repair while adding additional interest is the hard part and should be skipped when possible. Planning is a powerful tool to have on your path to financial happiness.

CHAPTER 19

CLOSING

Give a man a fish and you feed him for a day. Teach a man to fish and you feed him for a lifetime.—Chinese proverb

Thank you for reading my book. My wish is that when you close *The Little Green Book of Financial Happiness* you will have found it helpful in regaining control of your finances. You are now on a road that might be difficult and long. Enjoy your journey; beautiful things are found on the most secluded and untraveled roads, especially on a road to a small town called Emmaus.

Happiness and financial wellness are easy to attain. Make this book part of your everyday life: make notes in it while you clip articles and collect receipts; just use it and have fun with it.

Over the next few weeks you will come up with incredible ways to save money, cut expenses, and generate additional sources of income. Share your great ideas with all who will benefit from them. The craziest part is when you start helping others improve their lives by finding financial happiness. Our humanity shows us that we enjoy helping others.

You will see the light at the end of the tunnel. Financial happiness was within you before you even picked up this book. Let's get to work. I wish you the best of luck, joy, health, and hope—and of course financial happiness—in abundance.

Simply by recognizing your true financial situation, you can start dealing with the financial realities that you are going to experience in the next few years. Start by cutting expenses, saving every dollar you can, and eliminating or reducing expenses outside your earnings bracket.

I never said this program was going to be easy, but it will be well worth your time. It will give you a little peace of mind and allow you to sleep better at night.

Get the whole family involved. Avoid vices; if you are broke, the last place you need to be is in a casino or bar. Instead of going to the movies, rent or download a video, or go to the library or a park.

The final and most important aspect of the work is the reduction of your *ego* in the process. The ME-factor might have gotten you into your present situation. Let's start to study ourselves. Admit your flaws and seek help when needed. Help is available, so start searching and asking for it. Now is a good time to contemplate your faith and put some effort into prayer or meditation.

What if you do not share my faith or belief? Whether you are an atheist, a Muslim, a pagan, a Buddhist, a Hindu, a Christian, a Jew, or whatever, you are first a human. Our humanity tells us that we want to be happy, to love and dream.

I have a friend who is an atheist, a very smart and logical man. He constantly reads religious books and argues with me about God's existence. I have never been able to convince him that there is a higher power; I am just not that good. He has confessed that he wants to believe in something bigger than himself. I have noticed that even though he is an atheist, he is nondestructive. He is creative and is always attempting to help others. I have always wondered why. He and all of us must have goodness in our DNA. Man as a species is good. We want to do more than just survive. We want to be happy.

I thank you again for reading my book and allowing my thoughts on financial happiness to interact with yours.

I wish you success and financial happiness. May faith, joy, happiness, love, and hope flood your life.

Please send your comments, ideas, and opinions to www.thelittlegreenbook offinancialhappiness.com.

Additional forms are available for a free download on the website.

Now Make Your Budget!

Use all you have learned and set up your budget. Keep it simple. Keep it real. And enjoy your financial happiness.

My Budget

My Budget

My Budget

_____

_____

_____

_____

_____

_____

_____

_____

_____

_____

_____

_____

_____

_____

_____

_____

_____

_____

_____

_____

_____

_____

ABOUT THE AUTHOR

Raymar Rodriguez has been immersed in "everything money" since 1984. He was a banker at a large financial institution for twelve years. During that period, he had the pleasure of reviewing thousands of personal financial records, statements, profiles, and budgets. This training gave him the uncanny ability to quickly detect and address problems in his clients' budgets. He developed the Financial Survival Workshop, later called Financial Happiness Workshop, to address financial problems being experience by many in his community. The class is still being taught after ten years at his local church and through a career transition support network.

Raymar is passionate about all things money, education, international trade, and fishing. He holds a master's degree in finance and is currently an adjunct finance professor at Miami Dade College in his hometown of Miami, Florida. He is married and has three children.